PRESENTED TO

....

BY

....

ON

....

WHAT MAKES YOU BEAUTIFUL

20 Daily Devotions for Girls

KRISTEN WETHERELL

WHEATON, ILLINOIS

What Makes You Beautiful: 20 Daily Devotions for Girls

© 2025 by Kristen Wetherell

Illustrations © Hannah Green

Published by Crossway
    1300 Crescent Street
    Wheaton, Illinois 60187

All rights reserved. No part of this publication may be reproduced, stored in a retrieval system, or transmitted in any form by any means, electronic, mechanical, photocopy, recording, or otherwise, without the prior permission of the publisher, except as provided for by USA copyright law. Crossway® is a registered trademark in the United States of America.

Cover design: Erik M. Peterson

Cover and interior artwork: Hannah Green

First printing 2025

Printed in China

Unless otherwise indicated, Scripture quotations are from the ESV® Bible (The Holy Bible, English Standard Version®), © 2001 by Crossway, a publishing ministry of Good News Publishers. Used by permission. All rights reserved. The ESV text may not be quoted in any publication made available to the public by a Creative Commons license. The ESV may not be translated in whole or in part into any other language.

Hardcover ISBN: 978-1-4335-9248-5
ePub ISBN: 978-1-4335-9250-8
PDF ISBN: 978-1-4335-9249-2

Library of Congress Cataloging-in-Publication Data

Names: Wetherell, Kristen author
Title: What makes you beautiful : 20 daily devotions for girls / Kristen Wetherell.
Description: Wheaton, Illinois : Crossway, [2025] | Includes bibliographical references. | Audience term: Juvenile | Audience: Ages 9–12 Crossway | Summary: True beauty is more lasting than outer appearance, more valuable than worldly achievements, and more satisfying than people's adoration— Provided by publisher.
Subjects: LCSH: Girls—Prayers and devotions | Girls—Conduct of life—Juvenile literature | Girls—Religious life—Juvenile literature

---

Crossway is a publishing ministry of Good News Publishers.

RRD			34	33	32	31	30	29	28	27	26	25
15	14	13	12	11	10	9	8	7	6	5	4	3	2	1

To my daughters, Joanna Grace and Lydia Mae.
You are beautiful because you are his.

WHAT MAKES YOU BEAUTIFUL

What makes you beautiful, my dear?
What's in your heart? Why are you here?

Is it your eyes, your ears, your nose,
The face that your reflection shows?

Or what about your favorite shoes?
Your trendy clothes in many hues?

Is beauty based on what you see?
Or who you're turning out to be?

It's fun to wear your shoes and clothes,
To paint your fingers and your toes,
To play with makeup, do your hair,
To love what's lovely and to care
About your looks, how you appear—
But these things will not last, my dear.

When you grow old with hair turned gray,
Your outer self will fade away.
So beauty's more than what you see,
For looks will change and youth will flee.

But what about the things you do,
The gifts and work God's given you?

Is beauty found in being great,
In what you're able to create?

It's good to try to be your best,
To learn and grow, to make a quest
To realize all that lies within
And use the gifts that God's built in.
But—is beauty based on what you do?
Or what the Lord has done in you?

And what about your many friends,
The ones on whom you can depend?
Does beauty come from human love?
Or from the heart of God above?

It's wonderful to be desired,
Appreciated, and admired,
To know you're valued, loved, and prized
As being "someone" in their eyes.

But human love and fleeting praise
Will not compare to endless days
Of God's rejoicing and his smile.
(All else will only last a while.)

What makes you beautiful, my dear,
Is not your eyes, your ears, your nose,
The face that your reflection shows.
It's not about the things you do,
The gifts and work God's given you,
The risks you take, the friends you make,
Or beauty for pure beauty's sake.
It's not what people say or do—
But what God says is true of you.

For God says beauty is the art
Of loving him with all your heart.

He says that knowing him means more
Than all the knowledge you could store,
And all the places you could go,
And all the people you could know,
And all the pretty, lovely things
That you could wear, like diamond rings
And trendy clothes with all the frills—
For knowing Christ is better still.

What makes you beautiful, my dear,
Is that your God is whom you fear,
The one you follow all your days,
The one you love and trust and praise.

For he's the one who says, "You're mine,"
Who made you from his good design,
Who knows your thoughts and all your deeds,
Your longings, sins, and all your needs.

He knows what makes you really *you*!
He died and rose to make you new.

And when you offer him your heart,
Your God begins his work of art.
He makes your heart his home and throne—
A lovely place to call his own.

A NOTE FROM KRISTEN

Hello, beautiful one!

Do you know that I've been praying for you?

I wrote this book for *us* because I often wonder, *What makes me beautiful?* We females can get confused about what true beauty is, can't we? That's why I wrote this devotional—so we will grow in our understanding of what makes us beautiful, and of the most beautiful person in the universe: God.

This book is for us, yes—but it is all about *him*. The more we learn to marvel and wonder at his beauty, the more beautiful we will become. But I'm getting ahead of myself!

Each day's devotion is short and sweet, and begins with a one-sentence summary about the whole devotion—which I call a Beautiful Truth. You will read a portion of my poem, a short Bible verse, and some brief thoughts about it. To finish, there is a prayer and then a creative prompt to help you apply what you're learning. Each chapter offers you some journaling pages where you can write down your thoughts. You'll also notice some fill-in-the-blanks throughout the chapters to help you remember God's truth.

At the very end, you will find a list of books about true beauty. I've also included a Ten-Day Bible Reading Plan if you want to keep going. God's word is such a treasure!

I encourage you to share what you are learning with others, especially your parents. Did you know that talking about what you're learning helps you learn it even better? You might even ask someone to read this alongside you.

One more thing: grab a pen or pencil and, as you read, circle the word *heart* every time you see it. This will be a very important word! We are about to discover that while we can't change our own hearts, there is someone who can. He alone makes us beautiful.

I am continuing to pray for you, and I hope you enjoy this devotional!

Love in Christ,

Kristen

"Let your adorning be the hidden person of the heart with the imperishable beauty of a gentle and quiet spirit, which in God's sight is very precious."

1 PETER 3:4

DAY 1

THE HIDDEN PERSON
OF THE HEART

What makes you beautiful, my dear?

Every girl wants to be beautiful. (This includes older women, like me!) Isn't that why you're reading this? Something made you curious enough to pick up this book. Some part of you longs to know, *What makes me beautiful?*

How would you answer that question? What makes *you* beautiful?

Is true beauty defined by how you look? Is it based on the things you're good at doing? Is beauty about how popular you are or your social media followers or the friendships you have?

Our culture would answer, "Yes, yes, and yes!" The world tells us to find our worth and value—our beauty—in appearance, accomplishments, and relationships. It tells us to look within ourselves *and* to compare ourselves to others. We are even told by stores and social media that we can create the beauty we're looking for!

But deep down in our hearts, we know these things won't make us happy. They might make us feel beautiful for a moment, but the happiness fades. At the end of the day, what we long for is to be told "You're beautiful" *by someone who really matters*.

Our verse today tells us who that "someone" is: God, our beautiful Creator and Savior. "Let your adorning be the hidden person of the heart with the imperishable beauty of a gentle and quiet spirit, which in God's sight is very precious" (1 Pet. 3:4).

This verse tells us some important truths about beauty.

> *God sees everything about you.*
> "God's sight" is perfect. He sees and knows everything about you in the "hidden" place that really matters: *your heart*.

> *God says your heart matters most.*
> "The hidden person of the heart" is the center of what you love and it motivates everything you do. More important than how you look and what you're good at, God cares about what (and who) you love.

> *God wants you to have a beautiful heart.*
> God wants your heart to be filled with true and lasting beauty ("imperishable beauty"). A beautiful heart is "very precious" to him.

So, what makes you beautiful, my dear? God's word says we must start with your *heart*. What matters most to him is what he sees deep within you.

LET'S PRAY

Creator God, thank you for making me! You see my heart, and you know me. Open my heart right now to your word, that I may know and believe what makes me truly beautiful to you. In Jesus's name, amen.

LET'S CREATE

What are some things that are on your heart right now? Write them on your journaling pages. Here are some prompts to help you get started:

1. What do you think makes you beautiful?
2. When someone says, "You're beautiful," how does this make you feel?
3. What do you hope to learn from this book?

BEAUTIFUL TRUTH

God is my beautiful
Creator and Savior.

God is my beautiful Creator and Savior.

"He has put eternity into man's heart."

ECCLESIASTES 3:11

DAY 2

STAMPED FOR ETERNITY

What's in your heart? Why are you here?

"Why am I here?" is one of the most important questions any human being could ask. Do you exist to become famous, to accomplish amazing things, to make your beautiful mark upon the world? Or do you exist for some other purpose?

What do you think? Why are *you* here?

The world will invite you to pursue your own happiness and truth. It will beckon you to become all you can be. It will tell you that the purpose of your life—and what makes you beautiful—is mainly about *you*.

But what if you were made for more?

Our verse today says, "[God] has put eternity into [your] heart." Your heart was made for God, for eternity with him—for everlasting beauty in his beautiful presence. And this beauty begins here and now.

God made you, dear one, to *know* and *show* his beauty.

> ⁓ ***God made you to know his beauty.***
> Another word for beauty is *glory*. The Bible says that God is endlessly glorious—stunningly beautiful!—and that there is no one like him. Because he has "put eternity into [your] heart," you will be happy only if you are in a right and healthy relationship with your beautiful God.

> ⁓ ***God made you to show his beauty.***
> Because he is God—Father, Son, and Holy Spirit—he has everything he needs; he needs nothing from us. But amazingly he has delighted to share himself with us! He has made you to be a reflection of his glory to the world around you, a picture of his beauty.

The desire you have to be beautiful has been planted within you by God, the source of all beauty. You were made by a good, creative, generous, and perfect Maker who has stamped a most important message upon your heart: "You're mine. I want you to know and show my beauty."

This is why you are here. This is why God made you.

LET'S PRAY

Glorious and Beautiful God—Father, Son, and Holy Spirit—you have stamped eternity upon my heart. Thank you for giving me a purpose: to know and show your beauty! Help me to love you more and become more like you.
In Jesus's name, amen.

LET'S CREATE

On your journaling pages, write down this precious reminder and insert your name in the blank: "God made _____ to know and show his beauty." Our world tells us that beauty is found in the way we look, the things we accomplish, and the people who love us, but God tells us we exist for something better. What does this beautiful truth mean to you today? Write down your thoughts.

BEAUTIFUL TRUTH

God made me to know
and show his beauty.

God made me to know and show his beauty.

"You formed my inward parts;
   you knitted me together in my mother's womb.
I praise you, for I am fearfully and wonderfully made."

PSALM 139:13—14

DAY 3

WONDERFULLY MADE

What makes you beautiful, my dear,
Is not your eyes, your ears, your nose,
The face that that your reflection shows.

What is one of your favorite things about yourself? Don't feel hesitant—go ahead and think about this question!

You are God's special creation. He designed you before you were born, formed you as a baby in your mother's womb, and planned what would make you uniquely *you*. Because God is your Maker, you are incredibly valuable—all of you.

So far we have seen that God cares most about your heart, and that what makes you beautiful is knowing him and showing him to others. We will look more deeply at these truths in the rest of this book. But here's an equally important truth: your physical body also matters to God because he made *all* of you.

You can admire and care for your outer appearance in the right way because every part of you belongs to God, your heart *and* your body.

As today's verse says, he "formed [your] inward parts" and "knitted [you] together"—and you can praise him for this (Ps. 139:13–14). Your body is a part of God's good plan and purpose.

This means a couple of things for you:

— *You can praise God for the parts of you that you love.*
Maybe you love your eyes and your bright smile, your curly hair, or how tall you are. These are good gifts from God, and they are meant to show his beautiful glory. Rather than being prideful about these gifts, you can praise God for them!

— *You can praise God for the parts of you that you don't love.*
Maybe you don't love your eyes or hair, your body type, or the fact that you need to use a wheelchair. Do you know that your least favorite features are also meant to show God's beautiful glory? You can praise God for every single part of you because he doesn't make mistakes.

So, dear one, the next time you glance in the mirror, remember that you are incredibly valuable because God made all of you—your heart *and* your body. Remember that every part of you is meant to know and show his beauty.

LET'S PRAY

Good and wonderful God, I praise you because you made me in your image with value and worth. I am your unique, wonderful creation. Help me to praise you for the way you've made me. You don't make mistakes. In Jesus's name, amen.

 LET'S CREATE

On the journaling pages that follow, write about some of your favorite features that God gave you. Thank the Lord for the beautiful characteristics he has given you. Let this prayer remind you that God had you in his mind and created you to bring him glory.

BEAUTIFUL TRUTH

Because God is my Maker, I am incredibly valuable—all of me.

Because God is my Maker, I am incredibly valuable—all of me.

"Everything created by God is good, and nothing is to be rejected if it is received with thanksgiving, for it is made holy by the word of God and prayer."

1 TIMOTHY 4:4—5

DAY 4

ENJOYING GOD'S GIFTS

Or what about your favorite shoes?
Your trendy clothes in many hues?

"Mommy, why do you wear makeup?"

My young daughter asked this question as she watched me paint my eyes and decorate my cheeks with color. "I don't need to wear makeup," I told her. "But I like to sometimes. God gave us girls so many lovely features, didn't he?"

God has given us girls so many fun and beautiful gifts to enjoy, hasn't he? There's makeup, clothing, jewelry, shoes, hairstyles, accessories—the list could go on!

It would be easy to think, *If God cares most about my heart, then I shouldn't care about anything else*. We might start to believe that these "fun things" we enjoy are bad, and that we should not enjoy them anymore. But our verse today tells us the opposite: everything created by God is *good*, and there is a *good* way to enjoy his gifts!

What makes you beautiful? Not the way you look—but that doesn't mean God wants you to stop caring about the beautiful, good gifts he gives you. He wants you to thank him for them—shoes, clothing, and all!—and then use those good gifts in ways that honor him.

You can receive everything "with thanksgiving." So, the next time you get dressed or put on makeup (or enjoy any of God's good gifts), try thanking him like this:

— *"Thank you, God, for giving me good gifts to enjoy!"*
Take a moment to *know* God's beauty better through his gifts. Tell him that everything beautiful you have comes from him. When we are thankful, we give God the honor he deserves, and we draw near to him in our hearts.

— *"Help me, God, to honor you in the way I enjoy these gifts."*
Then ask God to help you *show* his beauty through his gifts. Ask him to help you use these gifts—makeup, clothing, jewelry, shoes, hairstyles, and accessories—in ways that point others to *him*, rather than to you.

LET'S PRAY

Good and Gracious God, I am so thankful for who you are and everything you give me to enjoy. Please help me to always thank you for these gifts and honor you in the ways I receive and use them. In Jesus's name, amen.

 ### LET'S CREATE

What are some of your favorite "fun things"? On your journaling pages, make a list of some of God's good gifts that you especially love. What would it look like for you to thank God and honor him as you enjoy these gifts?

BEAUTIFUL TRUTH

There is a good way for me
to enjoy God's good gifts.

There is a good way for me to enjoy God's good gifts.

"We all, with unveiled face, beholding the glory of the Lord, are being transformed into the same image from one degree of glory to another. For this comes from the Lord who is the Spirit."

2 CORINTHIANS 3:18

DAY 5

WHO GOD WANTS YOU TO BE

Is beauty based on what you see?
Or who you're turning out to be?

When I was little, I wanted to be a singer when I grew up. Or a veterinarian. Or a teacher. Or maybe a mom. My dreams changed all the time, but one thing was for sure: I knew I wanted to become different in some way, rather than staying the same. I wanted to grow up!

Have you ever wondered who *God* wants you to be? He wants you to be a reflection of his beauty—truly beautiful. Today's verse tells us that God wants to transform us into his image. This means he wants us to be like him, to look like him. Imagine becoming a mirror of God's beauty!

But we can't make this happen on our own. Who can help us? Fill in the blanks:

"This comes from the _____ who is the _____."

The Holy Spirit of God is the only one who can help us see how beautiful God really is. On our own we are blind to God's beauty. So we need his help to see his beauty, what the Bible calls "the light of the gospel of the glory of [Jesus]" (2 Cor. 4:4).

Who is Jesus? Jesus is God's Son. He is the Lord of all and the most beautiful person who has ever lived. Because he is God, his heart is perfect—without sin. He is also a man, and he perfectly *knew* God the Father's beauty and perfectly *showed* his beauty when he walked on earth as a human being.

Jesus was punished on a cross for our sins. Sin is anything we want, think, say, or do that does not reflect God's beauty. Sin is what makes us blind to our perfectly beautiful and holy God.

But there is good news. God opens our blind eyes to see his beauty! This is why Jesus came: to restore our beauty and our relationship to God.

God wants you to become truly beautiful as he is beautiful. So he gave you his Son, Jesus, who is the only one who can transform your heart by his Spirit, helping you see how lovely and glorious he really is. He is also the only one who can help you reflect God's beauty.

You don't need to wait until you're grown up to see his beauty. You can ask him for this gift right now.

LET'S PRAY

Glorious Lord Jesus, please help me to see how beautiful you are! Open my eyes by your Holy Spirit to see my need for you and how you rescue me from sin. Restore me to my Father, forgive all my sin, and transform me into your image. Thank you, beautiful Jesus! Amen.

LET'S CREATE

What do you want to be when you grow up, and why? Write your ideas on the journaling pages that follow. As you reflect on this, remember who God wants you to be: a reflection of his beauty.

BEAUTIFUL TRUTH

Jesus came to restore my beauty
and my relationship to God.

Jesus came to restore my beauty and my relationship to God.

"All flesh is grass,
 and all its beauty is like
the flower of the field. . . .
The grass withers, the flower fades,
 but the word of our God
will stand forever."

ISAIAH 40:6, 8

DAY 6

A BEAUTY THAT FADES

*It's fun to wear your shoes and clothes,
To paint your fingers and your toes,
To play with makeup, do your hair,
To love what's lovely and to care
About your looks, how you appear—
But these things will not last, my dear.*

What is your favorite season?

Mine is autumn. I love when hot summer days give way to milder ones, when the vibrant colors of the earth change into subtle, warm hues: orange, red, yellow, gold. Leaves that were once bright green begin floating down from their trees, and summer's flowers fade. Even the grass is eventually covered with a blanket of morning frost. Winter is coming.

No season lasts forever.

No earthly beauty lasts forever either. We love marveling at beautiful things, but just like "the grass withers and the flower fades," everything we see with our two eyes is fading away. This includes our bodies and appearance ("all flesh"), as well as every good gift we enjoy here on earth (like shoes, clothing, and everything else that's beautiful).

Earthly beauty will fade, but God's beauty will last forever.

This is what God wants us to see through our verse today: "The grass withers, the flower fades, but the word of our God will stand forever." He wants us to know that earthly beauty won't last forever. But what *will* last forever is a transformed, beautiful heart that knows and shows the beauty of the Lord Jesus.

Does this mean we shouldn't care about beautiful things? No! Just because the seasons change and fade doesn't mean we don't notice their beauty and care about them; and just because our earthly gifts and beauty will fade someday doesn't mean we can't enjoy them now.

Instead, our perspective changes. *Perspective* means that we start to care most about what matters most—in this case, a lasting beauty in our hearts that will never fade.

We also gain perspective about another beautiful truth from God's word. Those who love Jesus will gain resurrection bodies that will last forever! We will never grow old, never fade, and never die.

So yes, we should care about our outer appearance and love what's beautiful, enjoying how fun it is to decorate ourselves in beauty. This matters! But it's not *all* that matters, for these things will not last forever. They will all fade away.

But what will last forever, my dear? A transformed, beautiful heart that knows and shows the beauty of her Lord Jesus Christ.

LET'S PRAY

Beautiful God, please give me perspective today about what matters most as I care for myself and enjoy the good and beautiful gifts you've given me. Help me care most about what will last forever: a heart (and body!) that knows and shows your beauty. In Jesus's name, amen.

LET'S CREATE

Use your journaling pages to compose a short poem or song about true beauty (like the one from Isaiah). If it's a song, try putting it to music using an instrument you play.

BEAUTIFUL TRUTH

Earthly beauty will fade,
but God's beauty will last forever.

Earthly beauty will fade, but God's beauty will last forever.

"Though our outer self is wasting away,
our inner self is being renewed day by day."

2 CORINTHIANS 4:16

DAY 7

THE BEAUTY THAT LASTS FOREVER

When you grow old with hair turned gray,
Your outer self will fade away.
So beauty's more than what you see,
For looks will change and youth will flee.

Do you ever wonder what you'll look like when you're old?

Growing old is hard to believe, isn't it? Right now, there's not a gray hair on your head (unless you're wearing silver highlights!). Many people think aging is horrible. Think about all the anti-aging creams and makeup sold in stores. Our culture tells us that we get worse with age.

But believers in Jesus have a different perspective: we can get *better* with age! As reflections of God's beauty, we become more and more beautiful where it really matters—in our hearts.

Remember what we learned yesterday? Everything we see and enjoy here on earth will fade. Nothing here lasts forever—not our bodies or our physical features. But what *will* last forever? Read today's verse again, and fill in the blanks:

"Our _____ _____ is being renewed day by day."

Did you write "inner self"? "Inner self" describes our hearts. This hidden, unseen part of us is eternal, which means it will last forever. This verse is saying that believers in Jesus can get better with age! Even as our bodies turn old and gray and wrinkly, and even as our outer selves are wasting away, our hearts (our "inner selves") can become more and more beautiful.

But how is it possible to become more and more beautiful in our hearts if our bodies are fading away?

This is not something we can do on our own. No—*God* must transform us! Through his Holy Spirit, "our inner self is being renewed day by day." This means that God's Spirit makes us a reflection of God's Son.

But this doesn't happen overnight. Instead, day by day, little by little, the Holy Spirit causes us to see how lovely and glorious Jesus really is, and he changes our perspective so we care most about looking like him.

Dear one, God wants you to become *better* with age, where it really matters—in your heart!

LET'S PRAY

Dear God, I want my beauty to last forever! Make my heart a reflection of Jesus, one that knows and shows his beauty. Even as my body changes and fades, I want my heart to get better and better with age. Renew my inner self, Holy Spirit. In Jesus's name, amen.

LET'S CREATE

On your journaling pages, describe the kind of woman you would like to be when you're older. What character traits do you want to display as you age and mature?

BEAUTIFUL TRUTH

You can become more and more beautiful where it really matters—in your heart.

*You can become more and more beautiful
where it really matters—in your heart.*

"Whatever you do, in word or deed, do everything in the name of the Lord Jesus, giving thanks to God the Father through him."

COLOSSIANS 3:17

DAY 8

EVERYTHING FOR JESUS

*But what about the things you do,
The gifts and work God's given you?*

Have you ever tried to ride a unicycle? I can hardly stand on one foot, so I can't imagine how a person can balance on a bike that has only one wheel! The world record for the longest unicycle ride (without someone's feet touching the ground) is 106 miles—the length of 1,760 football fields. That's some talent!

What are some of your talents? Has God made you good at sports or dance or reading? Maybe you're a great listener and you're good at making friends. Maybe you love to do science experiments or cook meals for your family. God has given each one of us unique and beautiful abilities and many ways to use them.

We often think that beauty is about our looks, but we can also think it's about the things we do or accomplish. It's easy to believe that our value is based on what we're good at doing. But God's word tells us something different.

Do you remember what your God-given purpose is? On Day 2, we discovered that God made each one of us to *know* and *show* his beauty. God wants you to be a picture of his beautiful glory to the world—and this includes your abilities, gifts, and talents.

Fill in the blanks according to today's verse:

"Do _____ in the _____ of the Lord Jesus."

When you do something "in the name of" someone, you're showing or displaying what that person is like. We might rephrase this to say, "Do everything to show how beautiful Jesus is!" The amazing thing is that this truly includes *everything* you do—not just world-record-breaking talents like unicycle riding!

You can listen to your parents, grandparents, teachers, or pastors in Jesus's name by honoring them with your love. You can win (or lose) a competition in a way that honors Jesus, praising him instead of yourself. You can paint a picture or dance or run or play chess in the name of Jesus with thankfulness in your heart for these gifts. You can even wash dishes, clean your room, walk the dog, or mow the lawn in his name, displaying his faithfulness and service.

So, what makes you beautiful? Doing *everything* to display the beautiful glory of Jesus—using your abilities, gifts, and talents to show how great he is.

LET'S PRAY

Dear God, please use all my gifts, abilities, and talents to bring Jesus honor. I want to do everything to show how beautiful he is! Make me a picture of his beautiful glory to the watching world. In Jesus's name, amen.

LET'S CREATE

What has God made you good at doing? Cooking? Crafting? Writing? Music? Who could you teach with the gifts and abilities God has given to you? Use your journaling pages to reflect on the gifts God has given you and how you might use them to serve and help others. You might start with this prompt: "Thank you, God, for making me good at _____."

BEAUTIFUL TRUTH

Everything you do is meant
to show Jesus's beautiful glory.

Everything you do is meant to show Jesus's beautiful glory.

"It is God who works in you,
both to will and to work
for his good pleasure."

PHILIPPIANS 2:13

DAY 9

BEAUTIFUL GOOD WORKS

*Is beauty found in being great,
In what you're able to create?*

What makes you feel happy? Think of five things that make you smile.

Here are my five "happies": Light roast coffee in the morning. A rose-colored sunbeam streaming through the window. My kids' laughter. An uninterrupted conversation with my husband. A catnap.

Have you ever thought about what makes *God* happy? What do you think brings God pleasure and makes him smile? It's a good question, and the Bible gives us an answer: "It is God who works in you, both to will and to work for his good pleasure" (Phil. 2:13).

So, what makes God happy? Everything you do in the name of Jesus. Your beautiful good works bring God good pleasure and make him smile!

Here are two important things to know:

— *First, the things you do can't rescue you.*
We cannot become beautiful like Jesus by

ourselves. Only Jesus can rescue us from sin and restore our relationship to God. And only Jesus can transform our hearts by his Spirit and help us see how beautiful God really is! In other words, what we do can't earn God's good pleasure.

— *Second, beautiful good works are the result of your rescue.*
After Jesus saves us by grace, our beautiful good works tell the wondrous story of our rescue! Through the power and help of his Spirit, our God makes us able to do everything in the name of Jesus. These are our "good works," and they are the result of our rescue.

So the next time you compare yourself to another girl; the next time you wonder if anyone is noticing you; the next time you have to give up something big for something small; the next time you wonder if you're making any difference, remember: Everything you do in the name of Jesus is a beautiful good work. Your good works make God smile. And that is truly beautiful.

LET'S PRAY

Beautiful God, it is sometimes hard for me to believe that I make you smile and bring you pleasure—but help me believe it! By your Spirit, work in my heart to bring you honor in everything I do. I want my good works to tell your beautiful story. In Jesus's name, amen.

 LET'S CREATE

If you have trusted in Jesus and he has rescued you, how might your good works tell this wonderful story? If you haven't trusted in him yet, why not do that today? Use your journaling pages to respond to these questions.

BEAUTIFUL TRUTH

Your beautiful good works
make God smile.

Your beautiful good works make God smile.

"Whoever would be great among you must be your servant, . . . even as the Son of Man came not to be served but to serve, and to give his life as a ransom for many."

MATTHEW 20:26, 28

DAY 10

TRUE GREATNESS

It's good to try to be your best,
To learn and grow, to make a quest
To realize all that lies within
And use the gifts that God's built in.
But—is beauty based on what you do?
Or what the Lord has done in you?

When you think about people who have achieved greatness, whom do you think of? Movie stars? Musical artists? Presidents, kings, and other political leaders? Social media influencers?

In the world's eyes, being "great" is about power and influence. When people accomplish great things, we consider them beautiful and worthy of our praise. And this isn't entirely wrong. We want to rejoice in God's goodness being spread around the world. But we don't want to lose sight of what God says true "greatness" is.

What does he say? Fill in the blanks:

"Whoever would be _____ among you must be your _____."

Jesus says that true greatness isn't found in reaching our potential, becoming powerful people, or climbing to the top with our talents. No—true greatness is about becoming a servant.

What does a servant do? A servant *serves*. A servant uses her abilities, gifts, and talents to help others and build them up. She spends her life for God's good pleasure, not her own.

This can be tough stuff because service often means saying no to what we want and saying yes to what God wants. Service means rejecting the world's idea of greatness (which is all about *ourselves*) and embracing God's definition of greatness (which is about *others*).

But service is also joyful and freeing! Why? Because it's what we were made for!

God made you to *know* and *show* his beauty, remember? This was Jesus's purpose too: "The Son of Man came not to be served but to serve, and to give his life as a ransom for many." Even though Jesus deserves to be served, he gave his life to serve *us*—to rescue sinners through his life, death, and resurrection. Now, he wants to make you a servant just like he is, and *this* is what it means to be truly great.

Beauty is based not on what you do, but on what the Lord is doing in you: making you a servant like him.

LET'S PRAY

Lord Jesus, thank you for serving me by giving your life as a ransom and by sending your Spirit to beautify my heart. Make me a servant like you, and teach me what it means to be truly great in your sight. In your name I pray, amen.

LET'S CREATE

Journal about some ways that you could serve others this week. Could you help with chores at home? Mow a neighbor's lawn or shovel snow? Serve at your church? Pray for a friend? Ask God for opportunities to serve others, as Jesus has first served you.

BEAUTIFUL TRUTH

True greatness is about
becoming a servant.

True greatness is about becoming a servant.

"The Son of God . . . loved me and gave himself for me."

GALATIANS 2:20

DAY 11

LOVED INTO LOVELINESS

And what about your many friends,
The ones on whom you can depend?
Does beauty come from human love?
Or from the heart of God above?

I wish we could spend some time together so you could tell me all about you. I would ask about your family, your favorite subjects in school, the things you're really good at, and your hopes and dreams. I would also ask you to tell me about your friends.

What makes these friends special to you? Friendship is a wonderful gift from God. Our beautiful Creator and Savior made each one of us different and valuable. We have so much to learn from each other! God wants us to enjoy one another and show his beauty to each other. This is the purpose of friendship.

Now think about this: even your best friendship doesn't come close to God's friendship and love! Our verse today tells us that "the Son of God . . . loved [us] and gave himself for [us]" (Gal. 2:20). Fill in the blanks with your name:

Jesus loved _____ and gave himself for _____.
      [your name]   *[your name]*

Author Sally Lloyd-Jones, who wrote *The Jesus Storybook Bible*, says this about God's love for his people: "God saw all that he had made and he loved them. And they were lovely because he loved them."[1] (Read that again to really take it in.) In other words, you are lovely because you are loved by your beautiful Lord and rescuer.

A good friend is one you can depend on, right? You need to be able to trust your friends, and your trust in them grows as you see their love for you. Our verse today tells us how perfect and trustworthy God's love is. There is nothing like being called a beloved friend of God!

So when your friends disappoint you; when they are not faithful to you; when their love fails; or when you care too much about what they think, remember: You are lovely because you are loved by God's Son. His friendship is perfectly beautiful, and it's what makes you beautiful.

---

[1] Sally Lloyd-Jones, *The Jesus Storybook Bible* (Grand Rapids, MI: Zondervan, 2007), 25.

LET'S PRAY

Beautiful Lord Jesus, thank you for loving me and giving yourself for me. Help me to know, deep in my heart, how much you love me. Your friendship makes me beautiful. Help me to love you more and become a more loving friend. In your name I pray, amen.

LET'S CREATE

On your journaling pages, write a letter to a friend. Encourage her and tell her how thankful you are for her friendship. Then read it to her the next time you're together.

BEAUTIFUL TRUTH

You are lovely because you
are loved by God's Son.

You are lovely because you are loved by God's Son.

"How can you believe, when you receive glory from one another and do not seek the glory that comes from the only God?"

JOHN 5:44

DAY 12

SEEKING THE
GLORY OF GOD

*It's wonderful to be desired,
Appreciated, and admired,
To know you're valued, loved, and prized
As being "someone" in their eyes.*

Everyone wants to be loved, right? There's nothing wrong with . . .

- An audience's loud applause after your dance recital
- A teacher's kind words about your good grades
- A friend's compliment about your fun new haircut
- A parent's pride in your first-place trophy

It's wonderful to be admired by others! How does it make you feel when people compliment you or let you know they're proud of you?

— *There is a good and right way to receive people's love and admiration.*
Admiration from others probably makes you feel pretty great! Why did God create relationships? He wants us to enjoy one another and show his beauty to each other. Being loved by others is a beautiful thing, and we can receive their love as a gift from God.

— *But there is also a wrong way to receive people's love and admiration.*

We can care way too much about what people think of us, making people more important than God. We might even change the way we look or act because we want other people's praise and attention. We might think that being loved and accepted by others is what makes us beautiful.

Jesus calls this "[receiving] glory from one another" (John 5:44). Our verse today tells us not to seek our beauty in what others think about us. Why not? Because God's opinion of us matters most.

Only God's perfect love, shown to you in Jesus, makes you truly beautiful. Remember: you are lovely because you are loved by God's Son. And nothing can separate you from his love—not even what other people think of you.

So, the next time you feel super great about yourself because someone compliments you; the next time you feel pressured by friends to do something wrong; the next time you feel lonely and hungry for friendship; the next time you're tempted to find your happiness in the number of social media followers you have, don't forget: God's opinion of you matters most.

"Seek the glory that comes from the only God" rather than people's praise. The love and acceptance of Jesus is what makes you beautiful.

LET'S PRAY

Glorious God, I want to seek your love and praise, but I am so quick to believe that other people's love matters more than yours. Forgive me. Help me to care most about your opinion of me. Fill my heart with the love of Christ! In his name I pray, amen.

LET'S CREATE

What are some good and right ways to receive people's praise? What are some not-so-good and wrong ways? Journal your thoughts.

BEAUTIFUL TRUTH

The love and acceptance of Jesus
is what makes you beautiful.

The love and acceptance of Jesus is what makes you beautiful.

"You shall be a crown of beauty in the hand of the Lord . . .
    as the bridegroom rejoices over the bride,
so shall your God rejoice over you."

ISAIAH 62:3, 5

DAY 13

GOD'S FOREVER SMILE

But human love and fleeting praise
Will not compare to endless days
Of God's rejoicing and his smile.
(All else will only last a while.)

Have you ever been to a wedding? Maybe you've been a flower girl or have spent time with the bride as she got herself ready for her big day. A bride usually wears a beautiful white dress and decorates herself with jewels. This is a special celebration, and she wants to make herself lovely for her groom.

My favorite moment is when the groom finally sees his bride. Sometimes he cries tears of joy! He smiles and rejoices in her beauty, amazed that he gets to marry her.

Do you know that God is like that groom? Our verse today says that "as the bridegroom rejoices over the bride, so shall your God rejoice over you." All those who love Jesus will one day *see* him, and Jesus will be happier than the happiest groom on his wedding day!

As we learned yesterday, being loved by other people is a beautiful thing. There is a good and right way to receive their admiration. But at the end of the day, people's love and people's praise will not compare to God's praise over you. All earthly beauty will someday fade, and this includes the praises of your family, teachers, coaches, and friends.

But do you know what will last forever? God's rejoicing over his beautiful, glorified people.

The Bible says that one day Jesus will return. He will bring all his people (his church!) to live with him forever, just like a groom marries his bride. Guess what will happen? All the transforming work he has been doing in your heart (and in the hearts of all his people) will be finally finished! "You shall be a crown of beauty in the hand of the LORD" (Isa. 62:3). His church will finally be a *perfect* reflection of his beauty—truly beautiful in every way.

Guess what will happen? A few amazing things. One, he will renew all of creation. Two, he will transform our bodies to be like his glorious, unending, resurrected body. And three, all the transforming work he has been doing in our hearts will finally be finished!

Jesus will be so thrilled with his bride—with how he has restored our beauty and our relationship to the Father—that he will rejoice! "As the bridegroom rejoices over the bride, so shall your God rejoice over you" (Isa. 62:5). For endless days we will enjoy him smiling over us.

Can any person's praise compare to that?

LET'S PRAY

Glorious God, thank you for sending your Son Jesus to rescue me, and thank you that he will return to finish this work. When I am worried about what people think, help me remember that you will rejoice over my perfect beauty forever! In Jesus's name I pray, amen.

LET'S CREATE

Journal about a memory you have from a wedding. Describe the decorations, the ceremony, and how the bride looked. What does it mean to you that Jesus will rejoice over his bride?

BEAUTIFUL TRUTH

God will rejoice forever
over his beautiful bride.

God will rejoice forever over his beautiful bride.

"Sanctify them in the truth;
your word is truth."

JOHN 17:17

DAY 14

MADE BEAUTIFUL BY THE WORD

What makes you beautiful, my dear,
Is not your eyes, your ears, your nose,
The face that your reflection shows.
It's not about the things you do,
The gifts and work God's given you,
The risks you take, the friends you make,
Or beauty for pure beauty's sake.
It's not what people say or do—
But what God says is true of you.

Hello, beautiful one! Let's recap what we've learned so far. See if you can fill in the blanks (feel free to go back and use the devotions you've already read):[2]

A beautiful _____ is very precious to God.

God made you to _____ and _____ his beauty.

Because God is your Maker, you are incredibly _____—all of you.

Everything created by God is _____, and there is a good way to enjoy his gifts.

_____ came to restore your beauty and your relationship to God.

Even as your outward beauty fades, you can become more and more beautiful where it really matters—in your _____.

Your beautiful good works make God _____.

God's opinion of you matters most, and he will _____ forever over his people!

I'm proud of you, dear one! You've learned a lot so far about what makes you beautiful.

What do all these truths have in common? They have all come from the same place: the Bible. We call the Bible God's word because it is no ordinary book; it contains the words of our beautiful, glorious Creator and Savior (2 Tim. 3:16).

When you read the Bible, God is speaking *directly to you*. In other words, your beautiful God wants to talk with you! Isn't that amazing?

Some people today think the Bible is just a boring, ancient book of rules that doesn't really help us. But this is a lie. God's word is a precious and beautiful heart-transforming treasure. Why? Because God is alive, and his words are powerful! They are living and active, and he uses his words to change our hearts (Heb. 4:12).

Another amazing truth? The whole Bible isn't actually about us. It's about someone else—the person we were made for, the one who makes us beautiful.

The whole Bible points to Jesus because he is the point of the whole Bible.

Enjoying our Bibles is how we get to *know* God's beauty, and it's how God transforms our hearts to *show* his beauty. Jesus once prayed this prayer for all his people: "Sanctify them in the truth; your word is truth" (John 17:17). To sanctify something means to

---

[2] Answers: heart, know/show, valuable, good, Jesus, heart, smile, rejoice.

set it apart for a special purpose. That something—or someone—becomes special, a beautiful treasure. Jesus wants to make us truly beautiful through his beautiful words.

What makes you beautiful, my dear, is what *God* says is true of you. This is why it's so important for us to spend time listening to God by reading our Bibles, hearing sermons at church, and talking about his words with family and friends.

Beauty is based not on what people say or do, or the things you accomplish, or how you look; true beauty is based on God's true word. It's how he makes you truly beautiful.

LET'S PRAY

God of All Truth, I praise you for your true, eternal words in the Bible. Thank you for giving me such a treasure! Please use your word to transform my heart, making me more like Jesus. In his name I pray, amen.

LET'S CREATE

On your journaling pages, reflect on these questions:

1. How would you describe the Bible?
2. What is one way you might spend time listening to God this week?

BEAUTIFUL TRUTH

Your beautiful God wants
to talk with you in his word.

Your beautiful God wants to talk with you in his word.

"You shall love the Lord your God with all your heart and with all your soul and with all your might. And these words that I command you today shall be on your heart."

DEUTERONOMY 6:5–6

DAY 15

THE GREATEST (MOST BEAUTIFUL) COMMANDMENT

*For God says beauty is the art
Of loving him with all your heart.*

eady for a story?

Once upon a time, there was a rich young man who owned lots of stuff. That sounds great, doesn't it? But deep in his heart, the young man knew something was missing. He had heard about Jesus, who was performing miracles and teaching about God. So the man asked Jesus, "Teacher, what good deed must I do to have eternal life?" (Matt. 19:16).

How did Jesus respond? "Go, sell what you possess," he said, "and give to the poor, and you will have treasure in heaven; and come, follow me" (Matt. 19:21).

If you were the rich young man, what would you have done?

The Bible says the young man went away, sad. Deep in his heart, he knew he was made for eternity—for everlasting beauty in God's beautiful presence. But he didn't see God as beautiful enough, and he loved earthly things too much. He cared more about money and possessions than he did a lasting beautiful heart that loved God. So he walked away.

Oh friend, please don't walk away from Jesus! True beauty and highest joy are found in loving him, the beautiful one. This is what he commands because it is best for us: "You shall love the LORD your God with all your heart and with all your soul and with all your might" (Deut. 6:5).

But how is this possible? It's not—not on our own strength. We love earthly things (like the rich young man did) way more than God, and we need our hearts to be transformed. But who can do this transforming work within us? "With God all things are possible," Jesus says (Matt. 19:26).

Only God can help you love him as he commands you to love him. Only the beautiful one can make you truly beautiful where it matters most: in your heart.

Think about this: One day, you will stand before Jesus, and everything else you love will seem small compared to him. But can you imagine loving him with a perfect love? Can you imagine a day when nothing else will compete for your affections?

Until that day, we call upon God's Spirit to do what only he can do. We ask him to do the impossible. Will you ask him to help you love him?

LET'S PRAY

Beautiful God, you command me to love you with all my heart, soul, mind, and strength—with all of me! I confess that I don't love you as I should. Forgive me. Help me. Make my heart truly beautiful by filling it with love for you. In Jesus's name I pray, amen.

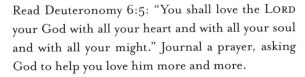

LET'S CREATE

Read Deuteronomy 6:5: "You shall love the LORD your God with all your heart and with all your soul and with all your might." Journal a prayer, asking God to help you love him more and more.

BEAUTIFUL TRUTH

True beauty and lasting joy
are found in loving God.

True beauty and lasting joy are found in loving God.

"I count everything as loss because of the surpassing worth of knowing Christ Jesus my Lord."

PHILIPPIANS 3:8

DAY 16

THE BETTER (AND BEST!) TREASURE

He says that knowing him means more
Than all the knowledge you could store,
And all the places you could go,
And all the people you could know,
And all the pretty, lovely things
That you could wear, like diamond rings
And trendy clothes with all the frills—
For knowing Christ is better still.

Ready for a pop quiz? Choose the more beautiful option in each comparison:

1. Pebbles or pearls?

2. Weeds or water lilies?

3. Trash or treasure?

This wasn't a hard quiz, was it? Many of us would agree that pearls are more beautiful than pebbles, and that water lilies are better than weeds!

Jesus once told a story about a man who discovered a treasure in a field. Do you think he would have wanted trash instead? No! He knew that what he had found was beautiful—better than anything else. So he sold everything he owned and bought that field (Matt. 13:44).

In our verse today, we see how nothing can compare with knowing Jesus: "I count everything as loss because of the surpassing worth of knowing Christ

Jesus my Lord" (Phil. 3:8). Christ is better and more beautiful than even the most lovely, wonderful earthly gifts!

So far, we've seen that what makes you beautiful isn't your outer appearance, your talents and abilities, or how well-liked you are by other people. All of these are good gifts—but none of them are better than having a relationship with Jesus, our beautiful King and rescuer. He is the only one who can change our hearts, and he says that knowing him means more than anything and everything else!

Jesus is our best and most beautiful treasure. Just like the man sold everything he owned to buy the field his treasure was buried in, we want to pursue knowing Jesus above all else. He is our beautiful reward.

How do we do this?

> — *We dig into his word, the Bible, where he speaks to us.*
> This is how we get to know Jesus better and grow in our relationship with him. We read and listen to his words just like we would spend time with a friend and listen to him or her.

> — *We talk with him through prayer, when we speak to him.*
> If you spent time with a friend but never talked to her, that would be odd, wouldn't it?

Jesus wants you to speak to him! He is a real person, alive right now in heaven, and he wants to hear from you. This is called prayer. You can talk to Jesus just like you would a close friend.

Knowing Christ is better than everything else, dear one. A relationship with him is what makes you beautiful.

LET'S PRAY

Jesus, you are my treasure! I want to know you. Speak to me in your word, and help me talk with you in prayer. I want to pursue you always, knowing that you are better than everything else. In your name I pray, amen.

LET'S CREATE

Write down a story about a time when you lost something valuable and then had to look hard to find it. Describe how you felt when you discovered it. What do you think Jesus means when he says that he is our greatest treasure?

BEAUTIFUL TRUTH

Your relationship with Jesus
is better than everything else.

Your relationship with Jesus is better than everything else.

"Charm is deceitful, and beauty is vain,
but a woman who fears the Lord is to be praised."

PROVERBS 31:30

DAY 17

THE RIGHT KIND OF FEAR

*What makes you beautiful, my dear,
Is that your God is whom you fear,
The one you follow all your days,
The one you love and trust and praise.*

What are some things you're afraid of?

I'm afraid of heights, so I refuse to ride roller coasters. I care way too much about what people think of me (what the Bible calls "the fear of man"), and I'm afraid to fail. Mostly, I'm afraid of the things I can't control.

When we hear the word *fear*, we usually think about scary things that we hope never happen to us. But did you know that there's another kind of fear—a *good* kind of fear?

The Bible calls this "the fear of the Lord." When we fear the Lord, we are amazed by his power and might, and this gives us the right perspective. He is God, and we are not! So we start caring about what matters most to him. Fearing God means we treasure him above everything else, listen to him, and spend our days knowing him and showing him to others.

What does our verse today tell you about what makes you beautiful? Fill in the blanks:

"A woman who _____ the LORD is to be _____."

A beautiful heart is a heart that fears the Lord, and only he can give you this beautiful heart. Earthly beauty—the way you look, the things you accomplish, the praises of people—won't last forever and will eventually fade. This is what our verse means when it says, "Charm is deceitful, and beauty is vain."

But someday we will stand before the risen Lord Jesus in all his glorious beauty, and everything else will be put in perspective. Remembering this day will help us grow in fearing him right now. We can also grow in fearing God by marveling at his amazing creation, reading his word to search out his character and promises, and taking all our other fears to him in prayer.

The things we see right now won't last. But what will last forever is a transformed, beautiful heart that loves, trusts, follows, and praises God. A heart that knows and shows the beauty of the Lord Jesus. A heart that fears him because it has been transformed by him.

LET'S PRAY

Lord God, teach me to fear you. I want to love you, trust you, follow you, and praise you with my whole heart. Help me believe that beauty is found in fearing you. In Jesus's name I pray, amen.

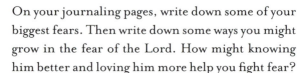 LET'S CREATE

On your journaling pages, write down some of your biggest fears. Then write down some ways you might grow in the fear of the Lord. How might knowing him better and loving him more help you fight fear?

BEAUTIFUL TRUTH

A beautiful heart is one
that fears the Lord.

A beautiful heart is one that fears the Lord.

"O Lord, you have searched
me and known me!"

PSALM 139:1

DAY 18

FULLY KNOWN, FULLY LOVED

*For he's the one who says, "You're mine,"
Who made you from his good design,
Who knows your thoughts and all your deeds,
Your longings, sins, and all your needs.*

I'm going to tell you a secret. Ready?

After my husband and I got married, we noticed that we had totally opposite bed-making habits. I like to turn down a neatly made bed every night, with the sheets tightly tucked around me. My husband couldn't care less about making the bed. He sleeps better when the sheets are untucked and messy!

This is a fun and silly example, but it makes a point about marriage: God calls husbands and wives to love one another . . . quirks and all! We see everything about each other—the beautiful and the not-so-beautiful—and we commit to love one another anyway.

Now, husbands and wives are not perfect, and neither is their commitment to one another. But God is perfect, and he makes a perfect commitment to you, dear one. God sees everything about you and loves you anyway. Our verse today says he has searched you completely—the hidden person of your heart. It says there is nothing about you that God does not already know. He knows your thoughts, your actions, your dreams, your weaknesses, your sins, and all your needs . . . every single one!

This means a couple of things for you.

— *You can't hide anything from God.*
God sees and knows everything about you in the hidden place that really matters: your heart. So why try to hide what he already sees? First John 1:9 says to tell God about everything, even the darkest parts of your heart. God says that when we confess our sins to him, he will forgive us. What a beautiful promise!

— *You can tell everything to God.*
Many of us have dreams we long for, outcomes we hope for, questions we want to ask God, and needs that we want him to provide. God wants to know everything that's on your mind. Nothing will scare him away. You can tell him everything and trust that he will never reject you or leave you.

Your Creator and Savior sees and knows everything about you—the beautiful and the not-so-beautiful—and is committed to loving you. Jesus's ultimate sacrifice is the proof of this. Now isn't that a beautiful thing?

LET'S PRAY

All-Knowing God, sometimes I worry that if people knew every part of me, they would not think I am beautiful. But you say that I am yours, rescued by Jesus! Help me believe that your commitment to me doesn't change.
In Jesus's name I pray, amen.

 LET'S CREATE

Write a letter to God. Use the journaling pages to talk to him about what's on your mind. Tell him what you love about him, the things you want or think you need, your failures and sins and questions, and the things you want to praise him for.

BEAUTIFUL TRUTH

God sees everything about you
and is committed to loving you.

God sees everything about you and is committed to loving you.

"If anyone is in Christ,
he is a new creation.
The old has passed away;
behold, the new has come."

2 CORINTHIANS 5:17

DAY 19

A BEAUTIFUL NEW CREATION

He knows what makes you really you!
He died and rose to make you new.

Caterpillars are fascinating creatures. I'll never forget the time we found a bright green caterpillar on our garage door. He was vibrant and lovely! That caterpillar would go on to make a warm chrysalis—its temporary home for ten days—and would emerge a beautiful butterfly with colorful wings. It would became a new creation.

We just learned that God sees everything about you—the beautiful and the not-so-beautiful—and is committed to loving you. God's love, however, won't leave you the same. He wants to change you! God wants you to be a reflection of his beauty, and he does this by making you a new creation in Christ.

Fill in the blanks for our verse today:

"If anyone is in _____, he is a new _____."

When Jesus rescues us from sin, we are transformed—like a caterpillar is transformed into a butterfly. God gives us brand-new hearts that love, trust, follow, and fear him. The "old you" passes away, and the "new you" is born!

That being said, a newly formed butterfly still needs to learn how to be a butterfly. Even though we have beautiful new hearts when we trust in Jesus, we still need to learn how to reflect his beauty.

This is what the Holy Spirit does as we read God's word and talk to him in prayer. He teaches us how to be truly beautiful, as Jesus is beautiful. We learn how to fear God, how to treasure him above all else, how to confess our sins to him, and how to praise and worship him for his forgiveness and love.

And someday soon, when Jesus returns to bring all his people home to a brand-new creation—a new heaven and earth—our transformation will be complete. The "new creation" he has begun within our hearts by his Spirit will be finished, housed within new, glorious resurrection bodies! We will fully and finally be everything God made us to be.

The world will tell you to "be yourself"—but we are actually most ourselves when we belong to God. He knows all you can be, and makes you really *you*! This is why Jesus came as a human (like you!), lived a perfectly beautiful life (for you!), died on the cross (in your place!), and rose in glorious beauty.

He did it to make you *brand new*. He did it to make you his beautiful creation.

LET'S PRAY

Beautiful Lord, it is hard for me to grasp that I am a new creation—but that's who you say I am! Help me believe it. Teach me to rely on your Spirit, and transform me into a reflection of your beauty. In Jesus's name I pray, amen.

LET'S CREATE

If you have been rescued by Jesus, what are some ways he has changed you? Journal about how you've seen him transform you into his image.

BEAUTIFUL TRUTH

Jesus came to make you
his beautiful new creation.

Jesus came to make you his beautiful new creation.

"If anyone loves me, he will keep my word, and my Father will love him, and we will come to him and make our home with him."

JOHN 14:23

DAY 20

YOUR HEART, GOD'S HOME

*And when you offer him your heart,
Your God begins his work of art.
He makes your heart his home and throne—
A lovely place to call his own.*

I hope you've enjoyed your time looking into God's precious word and learning what makes us truly beautiful.

How would you answer that question now? *What makes you beautiful?*

Now flip back to day one and look at how you answered that question. Has your answer changed at all? I'll bet it has—because God's word doesn't leave us the same. He changes us!

How? He makes our heart his precious home.

Jesus once said to his disciples that he and his Father would "move in" to their hearts. "We will come to [you] and make our home with [you]" (John 14:23). We make our homes with the people we love. And God makes his home with the people he loves, and with those who love him in return.[3]

Think of it: your heart—the precious home of Jesus! What an amazing gift! Think about Jesus "moving in" and decorating your heart with his beauty and glory (just like you have decorated your room with artwork, posters, lights, and colors). He longs to dwell with you and live in you through his Holy Spirit. He longs to make you his work of art—a living, breathing reflection of his beauty.

The truth is, until we see Jesus's beautiful face, you and I will struggle with knowing what makes us beautiful. We will glance in the mirror and care way too much about our looks. We will use our talents and care too much about achievement. We will listen to other people and care too much about what they think of us.

But we will also look to Jesus, and we will marvel at his beauty. We will be amazed, and we will be changed. We will become beautiful as he is beautiful. How? Because he is making our hearts his precious home.

He is preparing another home for us too. One day, we will enjoy our final and eternal home in the new heaven and earth, where Jesus himself will be our beautiful light.

Until that day, we wait and we worship. What makes you beautiful, my dear, is that your heart is God's home. Where God lives, his beauty shines. And where his beauty shines, he is honored and praised. This is what you were made for: to be truly beautiful as he is beautiful.

---

[3] I talk about this more in my book *Humble Moms* (Nashville: B&H, 2022). Feel free to tell your mom about this book!

LET'S PRAY

*O Glorious God, make your home with me!
I love you, Lord, and I'm so thankful that you
have loved me. Come to me by your Spirit, and
make my heart his lovely dwelling place. Help me
remember that what makes me beautiful is your
presence within me, both now and forever.
In Jesus's name I pray, amen.*

LET'S CREATE

On day one you reflected on some important questions. Revisit those journaling pages. How has God worked on your heart throughout this book? What have you learned? You might use these prompts:

1. What I've learned about God is . . .

2. What I've learned about myself is . . .

3. What makes me beautiful is . . .

BEAUTIFUL TRUTH

What makes you beautiful is
that your heart is God's home.

What makes you beautiful is that your heart is God's home.

BIBLE READING PLAN

Do you want to learn more about true beauty? Follow this ten-day Bible reading plan to discover more treasures in God's beautiful word. Read these verses by yourself, or grab a parent or friend to read with you. Some of them appear in this book, but it's always good to revisit what you have learned and go deeper.

A simple and good way to read Scripture is to ask a few questions about the verses you're reading, such as:

1. What does this tell me about God?
2. What does this tell me about myself?
3. How does this passage point me to Jesus?
4. What does this tell me about true beauty?
5. How does God want me to respond to his word?

Day	Bible Passage
1	Psalm 27:1–4
2	Genesis 2:18–25
3	Galatians 5:22–26
4	Psalm 139:1–16
5	1 Samuel 16:6–7
6	Romans 12:1–2
7	Proverbs 2:1–15
8	Isaiah 62:1–5
9	Revelation 21:1–4
10	Psalm 119:33–40

RECOMMENDED BOOKS
FOR GIRLS AND MOMS

Books about Scripture and Bible Studies

What to Wear: A Kids Bible Study on Looking Like Jesus by Catherine Parks (Moody, 2023). An eight-week study of Colossians 3 that encourages kids to "put on" their identity in Christ.

Unfolding Grace for Kids: A 40-Day Journey through the Bible (Crossway, 2021). A forty-day journey through the story of the Bible to help kids learn and love God's word.

The Radical Book for Kids: Exploring the Roots and Shoots of Faith by Champ Thornton (New Growth Press, 2016). A fun and hands-on exploratory guide to God's creation, his word, and the Christian life.

The Ology: Ancient Truths, Ever New by Marty Machowski (New Growth Press, 2015). A storybook that teaches kids about God and his word, teaching abstract concepts in creative ways.

Wonderfull: Ancient Psalms Ever New by Marty Machowski (New Growth Press, 2020). A storybook about a child and his grandfather making their way through the Psalms.

This Changes Everything: How the Gospel Transforms the Teen Years by Jaquelle Crowe (Crossway, 2017). A chapter book that shows us the difference Jesus makes in our hearts and lives.

Books about Beauty

Lies Girls Believe (and the Truth That Sets Them Free) by Dannah Gresh (Moody, 2019). An interactive book that covers twenty biblical truths young girls need to believe.

True Girl subscription boxes and events by Dannah Gresh. A monthly resource package that includes devotionals, stories, mom/daughter activities, crafts, and more: https://store.purefreedom.org/product/true-girl-subscription-box/.

Growing in Godliness: A Teen Girl's Guide to Maturing in Christ by Lindsey Carlson (Crossway, 2019). A chapter book that gives teens a path for growth in Scripture, the church, and holiness.

Girl Defined: God's Radical Design for Beauty, Femininity, and Identity by Kristen Clark and Bethany Baird (Baker, 2016). A countercultural guide to true, lasting beauty found in Scripture.

Creative God, Colorful Us by Trillia Newbell (Moody, 2021). An interactive look at God's purposeful design for a unified yet diverse people.

"Let your adorning be the hidden person of the heart with the imperishable beauty of a gentle and quiet spirit, which in God's sight is very precious."

1 PETER 3:4